VOICES FROM HOME

A Narration of Parents of First-Generation Migrants

WISDOM FROM OUR DIASPORIC ROOTS

EPHRAIM OSAGHAE MBL

Published by Tri-W Pty Ltd

Disclaimer: The information provided within this publication, including observations made and lessons learned, is of the nature of general comments only. While we try to keep the information up-to-date and correct, there are no representations or warranties, expressed or implied, about the completeness, accuracy, reliability, suitability, or availability with respect to the information, products, services, or related graphics contained in this publication for any purpose. Any use of this information is at your own risk. It is recommended that the reader obtain their own independent information and advice, where applicable.

ISBN (Paperback): 978-0-6484799-3-2

ISBN (eBook): 978-0-6484799-4-9

DEDICATION

To

Chief Jacob Enagbare Osaghae

and

Mrs. Grace Ailuelohia Osaghae

ACKNOWLEDGEMENTS

I would like to appreciate my wife, Esosa, and our children for their support. They have made life in diaspora a lot more meaningful. My thanks also go to my parents, Chief Jacob and Mrs. Grace Osaghae, for their time and attention while providing the narration for this book. Working with them on this project has further confirmed their wisdom with regards to issues of life. They have provided authentic voice from home. To my siblings and key members of my family tree, Shanti, Item, Murphy, Kenneth, Rex, Lilian, Edgar, Florence, Joy, Frank and Adesuwa, being connected with you gives me a great sense of belonging. We may be far apart geographically, but our links are strong and deeply rooted.

I honour Uncle Flakeson Aisueni for his contribution to this work. He provided validation for some of the historical information. I would like to also thank my sister, Joy, her husband, Frederick, and their children as well. They have been great co-hosts during the visits of Jacob and Grace.

Finally, I would like to thank my network of friends, colleagues, neighbours and community in Nigeria, my country or birth, and Australia, my country of residence. The rich learning experience of interacting with you over time has provided the inspiration and capacity for writing this book.

Table of Contents

1.0 Introduction and Background Information

'Writers live twice' - Natalie Goldberg

Key Words: Diaspora, Intending, New and Emerging Migrants, Wisdom, Voices from Home, Cultural Intelligence

So much has been written about the experiences of migrants and people of migrant backgrounds from various contexts – history, settlement, work and career, aging, etc. A previous publication by the author of this book, Ephraim Osaghae, is a reflective guide for a meaningful and whole-life migrant experience titled *A Handbook for Migrants: The Good, The Challenges and The Lessons*. He tried to bring some of the multiple perspectives into one holistic view. However, not many books present the viewpoints of parents of migrants and the significance of our roots - "voices from home."

Extended families are part of the key stakeholders in the conversations relating to migrant experiences and settlement as well as the overall intergenerational dynamics. They partake in the mixed experiences accompanying migration – the excitement of the decision to migrate, the emotional build-ups to the departure of their migrating loved ones, the disconnection, the losses, the pains, the benefits, and, overall, the whole migration experience and life in diaspora.

Migrants are part of family trees with roots that never die but, rather, extend far and wide with various ramifications for multiple stakeholders including the migrants themselves, their families (home and in diaspora), and the communities in their current country they now call home. There are various impacts of migration related to the family trees – the good, the challenging, and various lessons. This book highlights these impacts with the aim of providing insights which will be beneficial, not just for the current generation but, rather, the values are expected to transverse generations and the wider community as we continue to navigate the migration journey altogether. This book captures and presents the narration of these impacts in the form of stories, observations, and experiences of parents of first-generation migrants.

There are three main characters in the story of this book. Ephraim is the author and first-generation migrant living in Australia with his family of five including himself, his wife, and three children – sixteen, thirteen, and eleven years at the time of the publication of this book. Ephraim also has a sister, Joy, who lives in Australia with her husband and two children – eleven and eight years. Jacob and Grace are Ephraim's father and mother, respectively. They reside in Nigeria and have visited and had long stays with their first-generation migrant children (Ephraim and Joy) and their family units in Australia on two occasions. It was during one of these visits that Ephraim obtained valuable information via series of formal and informal interview sessions with Jacob and Grace. The data obtained have been supplemented with observations and relevant research. Contained within this book are words and viewpoints from loving and visiting parents of typical migrant families – the good, the challenges, and wisdom.

Some of the benefits and target beneficiaries from reading this book are as follows:

- This book provides resources, hints, and tips for intending migrants[1] as part of their preparations for their migration journeys even before they leave their countries of origin.

[1] Intending migrants are those that are planning or preparing for their migration.

- It offers valuable lessons and strategies for new and emerging migrants[2] including opportunities to learn, make necessary changes, and grow well in their migrant experiences.
- It highlights opportunities and challenges to established migrants[3] and enables them to further engage and enrich their communities; migrants must be at the forefront of efforts to support other migrants.
- It features key principles of hope, opportunities, and empowerment for migrant youths with the aim of motivating them to positively explore and value their roots as part of the efforts of being the best versions of themselves.
- This book also contains insightful recommendations to community leaders as they prepare to take their respective communities to the next level of sustainable growth.
- It provides local residents, students, service providers, and policymakers with information and multicultural intelligence for better understanding and support for migrants.
- This book informs global audiences on lived experiences of migrants starting with the Australian context.
- The book will recharge the (need for) value-adding conversations around identity, migrant roots, extended families,

[2] New and emerging migrants are those that are less than one year in the new country and are still trying to settle.

[3] Established migrants are those that have been in the new country and/or have settled reasonably well.

multicultural / intercultural intelligence, integration, and other socio-economic aspects of migration.

- It provides insights for readers and stakeholders on the key dynamics and interplay of cultures, underpinning motivations, and extended families of typical first-generation migrants.
- It provides hints and tips for new and emerging migrants on how to support family members back in their countries of birth.
- It should inspire more migrants to revisit their family trees and write their stories. The minimum value of publication of such story is that first, second, and subsequent generations would have documented accounts of their heritages and extended families.
- This book also provides lessons for parents and family members of migrants, as well as migrants themselves, on how to maximize the benefits of migration. This also includes avoiding the pitfalls, working together as a winning team, and turning the challenges into opportunities for growth and long-term benefits for all involved.
- This book will make further contributions in providing hints and tips for policy making, alignment, and implementation.
- The book serves as a legacy of Jacob and Grace. Yes, it is not just about them, but they have contributed to the content, inspiration and support for the book.

1.1 The Diasporic Narrative: *The Tension of the Middle*

People leave their homelands and resettle into new countries for various reasons. Some do this voluntarily, including for studies, skilled migration, family reunions, or investor-type migration, and they remain in the new countries as temporary or permanent residents initially, ultimately becoming citizens where applicable. On the other hand, there are people that are forced to leave their country of birth mainly due to economic hardships, natural disasters, wars, risk of unjust victimisation, etc. Thus, these people are awarded refugee, humanitarian, and asylum visas, depending on the cases. Again, many end up staying permanently and they take up citizenship. Of course, there are strict eligibility criteria for these visas, and they will vary for various countries as well, being highly dependent on the country of origin. Moreover, only a few reasons for migration and visa application types have been mentioned in this section. Thus, there are increasing number and diversity of people in diaspora – the spread of people from their original homeland.

There are increasing number and diversity of people in diaspora – the spread of people from their original homeland.

Irrespective of the diasporic pathway, everyone involved or affected by this dispersion has a story or two to tell regarding their experiences. What is yours? We readily want to share some, while we share others with caution or will rather keep some as secrets, understandably so. Some diasporic stories are relatively light to handle, and those may be the ones that are readily out there in the public domain. Other stories may be so traumatic that the tellers will require professional support to share them, and hopefully they do so especially to their benefit. Unfortunately, some may never be told or heard, regrettably so, especially if such stories would have had lessons and benefits for people.

The *tension of the middle* is one such narrative that is associated with migrants in diaspora. Firstly, many migrants have the hope and continuous affirmation that the current positions and future aspirations are better than remaining in their homelands, especially at the time and situation when they made the decision to migrate. However, there are also many that ponder over the question: have I made the right decision to leave my homeland and all that was associated with it, including my upbringing, my established network of

The tension of the middle is real; people in diaspora handle and cope with the situation differently.

family and friends, my culture, etc.? This question is more amplified during periods of challenges for people in diaspora. A few have even been more courageous in relocating back to their homelands (and sometimes with families). Unfortunately, many of them have returned to their new countries for various reasons. One of the common reasons is the inability to cope with the lesser standard of living in their homelands, especially after they have experienced life in a more advanced setting, including reliable utilities, dependable infrastructures, higher level of security, etc. The other common reason people return to living in diaspora is the fact that children of migrants could not cope with the change of living in the country of birth their migrant parents; many of them are born in diaspora and they are already familiar with the lifestyle therein. It is worth presenting one final reason why migrants in diaspora that attempted to relocate to their homeland have returned to the new country: They realized that there have been significant shifts, especially regarding network of family and friends, lifestyle, and culture. Families and friends have moved on to other relationships and countries themselves, and the lifestyle is no longer as they had anticipated. Many times, they may become even more lonely themselves. It is like ***reverse migration,*** and they would require going through the same sorts of struggles that have triggered their actions to relocate back to their homeland in the first instance. Refer to the author's book *A Handbook for Migrants: The Good, The Challenges, and The Lessons* for more points on these challenges and some lessons that could help with such decisions. Thus, in many cases, they come back and settle back into their new country and begin to work towards a better future for themselves and their families. However, the questions hardly ever go away: could we have been better off staying back in our homeland (especially with voluntary migration)? How do we maximise the vast opportunities in our new countries as we settle in and integrate better?

We must continue to encourage and facilitate value-added conversations about the tension in the middle. The vast benefits will include, but are not limited to, finding more sustainable solutions to the problems associated with the tension, helping people in diaspora to settle in better into their new country, and fostering more robust multicultural communities, where applicable. Some *wisdom from home*, via parents of first-generation migrants, can absolutely contribute to these efforts.

The concept of reverse migration is a borrowed phenomenon in bird migration (Wikipedia.org) where a bird will fly in the opposite direction of its species during migration time.

1.2 Why Wisdom from Home?

Wisdom could be considered as *doing the right thing and doing it rightly*. This is the author's perspective and it is based on experiences, observations, and consultations over the years. Wisdom involves a consideration of not just what we do, but how we do it. Thus, one can do the right thing, but wrongly and vice versa. It is indeed very challenging getting this right most of the time, but the benefits of trying are worth the efforts. Consider this common example: is it wise to discipline a child in a way that leaves an injury – physical and/or emotional? Now, it is okay to discipline bad behaviour as a parent. The *why* is not in question, hopefully. But the **how** this is done matters a lot, sometimes even more than the ***what*** and ***why***. Now, the author is not a trained psychologist, neither does he boast having attained excellence in parenting. This has merely been used as an example that most people can relate to, especially in the family context.

Wisdom demands that we try more often to get the right balance of the why, the what, and the how.

Now back to why wisdom from home is important for people in diaspora; in other words, parents, grandparents, and/or ancestors contributing to why and how their descendants do what they do even in their new country of residence. One immediate statement to make here is this: all wisdom being proposed or suggested in this book must be within the boundary of the law. The author is also aware of circumstances where there could be conflicts between the laws and norms in the new country of residence of people in diaspora and those of their homeland country. All attempts would be made to avoid contexts that will require legal interpretations in the remaining part of this book, as the author does not have the capability or licence for interpretation of laws.

All wisdom and cultural norms must be applied within the boundary of the law.

However, the importance of wisdom from home can be illustrated by the concept of the family tree (see Figure 1). It is reassuring that most people, including migrants in diaspora and other readers of this book, can relate to the concept of a family tree. In the context of this book and with the illustration represented in Figure 1: Kurdy and Ada are parents of Jenny, Gina, and Johnbull. Gina now resides in Australia and is a single mother of three children – Steve and Tony (twin boys, 15 years) and Amina, 11 years. The twins were only 2 years when they migrated and Amina was born in the new country, Australia. Jenny still resides in their homeland country, along with their parents. Johnbull resides in Canada. Thus, Kurdy and Ada are parents of first-generation migrants Gina and Johnbull and grandparents of first- and/or second-generation migrants (Steve, Tony, and Amina), depending on which migration classifications you go with (to be discussed in a later section of this book).

Figure 1: Family Tree Illustration (names are not real)

Migrants in diaspora (like other human beings) are part of a bigger family which can be represented by the family tree like the one shown in Figure 1. We have roots which extend beyond places and cultures of our current country and residence. Whether acknowledged or not, we, along with what, why, and how we do what we do, are fed via the tree (ultimately, from the roots). Yes, we learn new behaviours along the way (hopefully, mostly positive). However, our roots still weigh a lot into our everyday living irrespective of our current places of abode. Hence, the concept "root cause analysis" is increasingly acknowledged as best practice in workplaces, medical contexts, etc. Basically, it means looking beyond the superficial in approaching an issue, experience, or action to explore the underpinning or underlying factors (the roots) holding what's seen, heard, and observed depending on the context. For example, how much does (and should) Amina know about her aunty Jenny, and her cousins, if Jenny has her own family back in the homeland as well? Would relating more with them providing her with the opportunity to know her roots (and herself) a bit more? Does this not bring up the hot topic of identity (and the escalating issue of identity crisis amongst people of migrant

Our roots still weigh a lot into our everyday living irrespective of our current places of abode.

backgrounds, especially younger generations)? What are the benefits of knowing and identifying with your roots (and, really, yourself)? At what cost/benefits should this be facilitated and/or enhanced by all stakeholders – the individuals, families, communities (and their leaders), schools, government, etc.? Of course, so much would be driven by the value placed on such relationships and/or the cost of inaction.

Unfortunately, while so much good can come through our family trees, "bad stuff" can, as well. The focus of this book is wisdom – doing the right, the right way – from our roots as migrants in diaspora. Wisdom from home. Wisdom from our ancestry and heritage. It is not just about what is inherited (like skin colour, accents, facial looks, etc.), but rather we can actively tap into that wealth of resources in our roots – for good. Yes, while the author may touch on instances of challenges associated with the diaspora, the ultimate emphasis is fostering useful lessons, or in this case, wisdom, for the good of all including the new communities that have embraced the people in diaspora.

Many migrants, irrespective of the generation, at one period or another, are like wandering spirits looking for settlement, for identity, for meaningfulness, for a sustainable future. The periods of this search are longer for some than others, depending on so many other factors. Yet, this breed of the human family must be commended for the courage and determination to take risks and actions necessary for survival for themselves, their families, and, often, for their bigger family trees that extend back to their homelands. But at what cost? Like most other things in life, diasporic journeys have their benefits and costs. Notably, these benefits and costs are intergenerational. Wisdom will help to maximise the benefits and minimize the costs. Such wisdom (at least part of it) can come from home – our family trees, our roots.

Specifically, wisdom from parents of first-generation migrants can be very instrumental to helping with settlement of the migrant families in their new countries. After all, they are key stakeholders in the wellbeing of their children and descendants however the distance, the time difference, and their emerging cultures in the new countries. This book is centered around sharing the wisdom based on the narration of parents of first-generation migrants in Australia whose homeland is Nigeria, a country located in the western part of Africa.

Wisdom from our roots can be very helpful with sustainable settlement of migrant families.

There is validity in the question of whether the lessons from the narration of Jacob and Grace are generalizable across all migrants in diaspora, including those outside Australia. Indeed, the author does not claim, and he has no intention to argue, that the wisdom shared in this book will apply equally across all diasporic contexts. Rather, there are principles and lessons in reading this book that will provide, or add to, the wisdom of most of the stakeholders involved with migration and people in diaspora. Hopefully, this contributes to the value-added narratives and conversations about people in diaspora – including the viewpoints of countries of origin, countries of destination, and the system in between. The deepest aim of the author is that readers, especially migrants themselves, will obtain and gainfully apply the wisdom presented in this book.

1.3 How to Read and Use This Book

The contents of this book contain narratives based on first-hand observations, experiences, and reflections of parents of first-generation migrants supplemented with diasporic research information and lived experiences. Readers will obtain the most benefits by reflecting on what is being read. Thus, there are supporting text boxes at relevant sections of the book which could further help to trigger such reflections. Read, reflect, record, and run with actions as per your objectives for reading.

The author's own objective is not to provide a prescriptive set of information or "how to live in diaspora," etc. Indeed, the author is aware that experiences vary across people of migrant backgrounds. Rather, one of the key intentions is to present some useful principles that are applied most of the time, for most of the target audience, and across most contexts. The book is aimed at triggering reflections and conversations around the subject of sustainable diasporic experiences. It is also meant to foster the necessity, courage, and maturity to go deeper to the "roots" in order to identify root causes, and sustainably resolve issues relating to live experiences of people in diaspora. The book also brings in the perspectives of parents of first-generation migrants into the conversations. After all, they are well positioned to provide guidance regarding our roots, especially for the benefit of second, third, and later generations of people of migrant backgrounds. Thus, readers can read the content and apply aspects that are relevant to them and their situations.

For intending migrants: it will be useful to reflect on key aspects of the book relating to challenges that migrants and people in diaspora face regularly, and some wisdom in this book can help with preparations for migration. This presents an opportunity to learn and avoid mistakes that many have made already, as well as avoids or reduces associated consequences and pains which are mostly generational as well, if unchecked.

For new and emerging migrants: take the same approach as intending migrants except that your case is not about preparations to migrate. Rather, it is about taking the next decisive steps to ensure that you set up yourselves and your families to lead meaningful and well-rooted whole-life experiences in your country of residence. This book can also be used as resource material for small group sessions for new and emerging migrants. It can assist with facilitating real conversations about the various topics and in masterminding sustainable settlements.

Community leaders of people of migrant backgrounds will find the entire book very useful as well. They must be champions of leading such conversations within their communities. Well-rooted members of such communities will more likely reflect in stability for that community and the wider community as well.

Local residents, students, service providers, business leaders, people managers, and policymakers can read, reflect, and develop the necessary multicultural intelligence and skills which have become increasingly in high demand considering the globalisation in neighbourhoods, schools, communities, workplaces, the marketplace, and policy-making. The escalation of the importance of roots of people of migrant backgrounds in this book will provide a real perspective for engaging in sustainable multiculturalism. The more we seek to understand, the more we learn about our differences, the more we learn to appreciate each other, the more we celebrate the wealth of diverse cultures, the more we live in harmony. After all, we all have our roots. We all have blood flowing in our veins. This book adds to the hope for sustainable multiculturalism.

Reflection 1.0:

- What do you think about the concept of The Tension of the Middle? Do you think it applies only to migrants? Do you know cases like that – relating to yourself, friends, neighbours, etc.?

  ____

  ____

  ____

- Who should be helping to sort out the issues associated with Tension of the Middle? The migrants themselves? Governments at country of birth? Governments in the new country? Community leaders? Etc. Why? How?

  ____

  ____

  ____

How would you describe wisdom (in your own words)?

____

____

____

2.0 Jacob & Grace: Parents of First-Generation Migrants

'No matter how far we come, our parents are always in us.'

— Brad Meltzer

Key Words: Parents of First-Generation Migrants, Jacob and Grace, Family Roots, Diaspora

Sometimes, it takes being far away from 'home' to appreciate the importance of family in our lives. Indeed, we often then realise that we may have taken the irreplaceable care of the family unit for granted. This is particularly challenging for people in diaspora that have migrated to a new country of residence with no family members. They would miss family members more than they had anticipated. Some would miss the family dinner time. For others, it is the fond and 'I got your back' type of friendship with cousins and extended family members. Yet, for others, it is the 'safety' and wise counsel in the company of parents.

Presented next, are a couple of sections introducing Jacob and Grace, including brief accounts about their early childhood experiences, education, how they met, romance and marriage, their children – at home and in diaspora – and, finally, their connection with Australia.

Figure 2: Jacob and Grace

2.1 Family Roots and Early Childhood

Jacob was born to the Osaghae family in Uhi in Uhunmwonde LGA near Benin City in Edo State, in the Southern part of Nigeria. See Figure 3 for map of Nigeria showing the location of Edo State. Nigeria is in the western part of Africa as shown in Figure 3 as well.

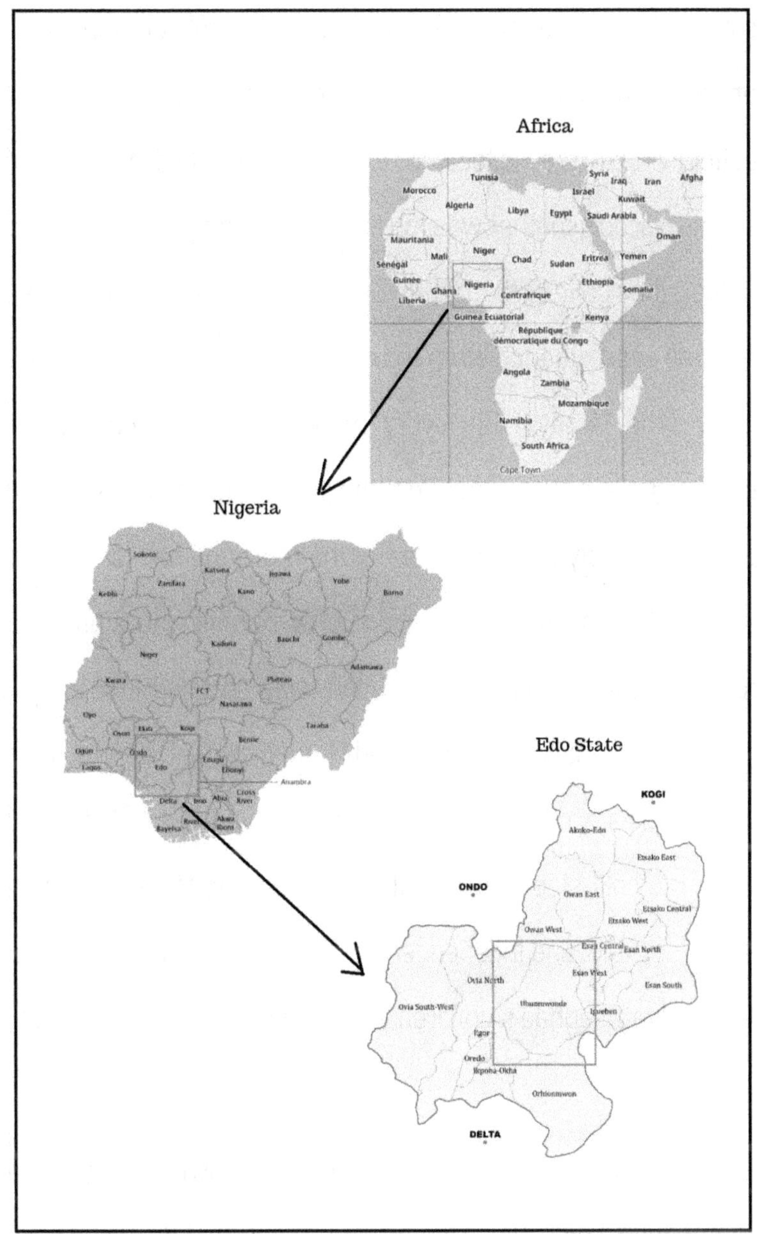

Figure 3: Maps of Africa, Nigeria and Edo State

Jacob's father was a farmer mainly cultivating rubber plantation and later moved to Obazagbon (another couple kilometres away) in search of better living. There, he took up residency and settled into his farming business. Jacob's mother was from a neighbouring village called Emu. Together, they gave birth to Ebun, Omoruyi, Festus, and Jacob. Jacob's father had eight other children from other wives with a total of twelve children. The family had a very modest living standard with full dependence on the proceeds from the peasant farming of their father, Osaghae. The polygamous nature of the marriage and family context resulted in the unavoidable situations of favouratism, lack of adequate care for all children, limited education for a selected few, and other circumstances. All these contributed to conflicts that were associated with Jacob's early childhood and upbringing even up to adulthood until he took the bold step to depart the home village to search for more sustainable work and independence. Jacob is the only surviving child of the twelve Osaghae's children at the time of the publishing of this book.

Grace was born in a village called Ugiamwen in the same Uhunmwonde Local Government Area, also in Edo State. Grace's parents were named Aisueni and Iyuwa. Her uncle (Aisueni's brother) was the Enogie (King) of Ugiamwen. Thus, Grace is part of the royal family. Her mother, Iyuwa, had fourteen children prior to Grace, but most of the children died due to illnesses and lack of adequate and affordable medical care. Grace was also born a very sickly child, but she survived. She and four other siblings eventually survived past early childhood – Samuel, Peter, Cecilia, Grace, and Flakeson. In her own words: 'I was destined to live." Grace and Flakeson are the surviving children of Aisueni and Iyuwa at the time of the writing of this book.

2.2 Education

Jacob was not as fortunate to enjoy a smooth educational experience. He undertook a bit of secondary education at a relatively more matured age due to lack of opportunities and sponsorship. Even that was short-lived when the financial situation in the family forced him to abandon his education to return to working on the family rubber plantation farm.

The desire and determination to obtain a high-quality education was sown in Grace at a very early age. She pursued this dream despite the difficulties associated with her upbringing at that time. There was lack of reasonably good schools in her village. There were literally no positive peer influences, no role models, and no mentors in her immediate and extended families, network of friends, and the entire village at that time. Finally, and maybe most significantly, her father and the elders of the family did not see the value in education, especially for a female child, and the expectation was for Grace to help her mother with housework and get married at the appointed time. Grace's father was not to be blamed; it was more of a cultural norm at that time. The limit was primary education for Grace. She took that opportunity, however limited, and commenced her primary education in 1950 in one of the local village schools. But Grace would not be stopped. Thankfully, she also had an ally for her bid to chase her dream of a high quality-education – her brother, Peter. With Peter's help and network, Grace proceeded to commence her secondary education in a teaching college in Akure, another state in the Western part of Nigeria.

Grace went back to the village during one of the school breaks. She rode in with her new *Superb* bicycle which her brother, Peter, bought for her. Her triumphant return had a great and positive impact on family and friends. Her dad was repentant and realized that Grace did the right thing after all, and her friends were challenged to pursue their dreams as well. Unfortunately, she fell ill during this same trip back to the village. What should have been a fever with an easy fix turned out to be a crippling illness that threatened her capacity to go back to school in Akure. It was locally diagnosed by a native doctor as caused by witchcraft and was dealt accordingly – in a native way, without the intervention of medical doctors/hospital treatment, which were not available anyway. The alleged culprit was uncovered, she confessed to the nocturnal act, and faced the *consequences*. Grace made a full recovery and went back to school in Akure. She completed her studies and qualified as a teacher.

This part of Grace's narrative was included in this book to make a point or two. Some people, like Grace, believe witchcraft and similar stories of 'black magic' are real. Others consider them as mere myths. The more specific question is this: would migrants with upbringing in a culture where beliefs in witchcraft are prevalent, and who may have once shared such beliefs, still be sharing such convictions? After all, we started this chapter with this quote: "No matter how far we come, our parents are always in us" by Brad Meltzer. Is it perceived as out of date in more advanced countries? Is it limited to the sphere of spirituality? However, there is an increasing recognition of spirituality even in what used to be traditionally academic disciplines including psychology, etc. These few questions are valid for further reflections. Back to Jacob and Grace.

2.3 Meeting, Romance, and Marriage

During Grace's study at the teaching college in Akure, Jacob was also a transport assistant 'conductor' with AMES Transport with frequent business along the route of the college road. The main driver and Jacob would pick up passengers, including students in the teaching college. In most of the cases, the college students would either be going from school to their homes, shops, parties, etc., as well as the reverse. Jacob and Grace met frequently during these transactions as driver assistant and passenger respectively. It was Jacob's act of kindness that brought the spark of love and attraction. Jacob noticed that one of his passengers (Grace) would always react to the fumes from the transport vehicle and this would cause her to exhibit symptoms of nausea and she vomited during the trips. Jacob took it upon himself to identify and make room for the best spot in the vehicle for Grace to occupy during the journey in such a way that the impact of the fumes was minimized and this resulted in Grace vomiting less and having more enjoyable journeys in the company of Jacob's vehicle. Grace would lighten up whenever she recalled these acts of kindness during the narration of her story that contributed to the manuscript for this book. Jacob, on the other hand, also recalled that Grace's modesty was a major attraction for him during the encounters of the trips. Her other friends would be more forward and visible, but Grace would always be in the background presenting a quiet and modest approach. However, it was all business at that time and there were no resulting dates or romance.

On successful completion of her teaching college education, Grace commenced her teaching career in Ekpoma, Edo State, closer to her home village. She performed her teaching duties to the best professional level at that time and received numerous acknowledgements and promotions along the way. But one reward that had stayed very close to her heart was her successful enlistment and participation in a beauty pageant where she earned the title "Mrs. Nigeria."

Figure 4: Grace as a Miss Nigeria Contestant

Back in the early days of her teaching career, Grace saw an advert in one of the national newspapers asking for expressions of interest to compete in a Mrs. Nigeria beauty pageant. She decided to have a go. She sent in her picture as required. She was not only selected to represent the whole of the Mid-Western part of Nigeria, but her picture was used for a front-page advertisement for the upcoming beauty pageant. That was how beautiful she was, and still is! She attracted the attention of Helen Enahoro (wife of the famous politician, Anthony Enahoro). Helen took it upon herself to personally and formally dress and provide mentoring support for Grace even though they were complete strangers at that time. The beauty competition took place in Obisesan hotel in Ibadan. She didn't win but she was given a gift and commended for her efforts and placing during the competition. Grace is still referred to as "Mrs. Nigeria" to date.

Meanwhile, Jacob went on to become an official head for a major political party in Edo State about the same time Grace was teaching in the same state. They were not too far from each other in terms of distance, but they did not know this. They eventually met again in the neighbourhood and it did not take too much time and effort for the memories of their previous encounters to spark love and romance between them, and they went on to formalize their marriage.

Figure 5: Jacob and Grace back in the early days

Typical for the culture in an African context, selected elders in Jacob's family met with Grace's parents and family elders to ask for Grace's hand in marriage. This was initially met with resistance, as some influential members of Grace's family had an expectation and set profile of a suitable husband for Grace – educated, wealthy, or, even better, both. However, Grace's insistence that Jacob was the man of her dreams and love paved the way for the marriage to proceed.

2.4 Children and Migration

The difficulty in securing the agreement of Grace's family for their marriage to continue was not the only challenge faced by Jacob and Grace. There was also the challenge of lack of adequate cash flow due to irregularity of Jacob's job. That resulted in moving from one region to the other as Jacob pursued opportunities for his career as a professional driver. Grace had put her family as priority, hence she did not settle into a fixed teaching contract, but instead she moved with Jacob from job to job like 'nomadic' living. Jacob's brother, Rev. Frederick Osaghae (now deceased), came to the rescue. Firstly, he provided financial support for Jacob to buy his first fully owned car for his transportation business. He also provided him a place to live in his house at 7 Osaghae Lane, Benin City, prior to Jacob's capacity to procure his own apartment. What started as a temporary residence became more permanent for Jacob's family, especially Grace and her children, who called it home for about 15 years. Jacob was mostly out and about pursuing his driving career. Rev. Osaghae continued to provide care for Jacob's family during periods of his absence, which was regular and lengthy due to the nature of his work.

There was also tension as a result of Jacob's extramarital affair, which he attributed to Grace's nagging torment that pushed him into the situation that ultimately resulted in a polygamous marriage and all the resulting tensions for the whole family over the years. There was obviously an increasing lack of care by Jacob compared to the acts of kindness that drew them together in the first place. Indeed, the emotions and acknowledgment of missed opportunities to continue in that love and modesty were evident during the narration for this book. These principles never die.

It was right during these tensions in their marriage that the author of this book, Ephraim Osaghae, was born. Ephraim is the fourth child of Grace – Shanti, Item, Murphy, Ephraim, Edgar, and Joy.

Figure 6: Grace and her Children during the Celebration of her 70th Birthday

My other siblings that are not Grace's children are Kenneth, Rex, Lilian, Florence, Frank, and Adesuwa. The dynamics of living within a polygamous family deserves a book of its own, so we leave details of that aspect from this book. But it suffices to state that it comes with its fair dose of fond memories, challenges, and lessons. However, the significance of names, and specifically the author's name, Ephraim, is one topic that will not be left out. In view of the context of this book, the key point is that names, naming, and impact thereof, are very important for families and cultures. Refer to the author's other book *A Handbook for Migrants: The Good, The Challenges, and The Lessons*, where he delved a bit more into career-related situations that have forced (and are still forcing) migrants and people of migrant backgrounds to change their names in order to make it easier to secure a job or other related opportunities while in diaspora. Just as the point was made in that book, one should not rush to pre-judge anyone under this circumstance – the person that changes his or her name, government, employers, or even the community. It is what it is, and the responsibility rests more with the person that has the name. Hopefully, they would have considered the pros and cons – immediate and long term – of such action.

Indeed, have you ever wondered what is in a name? Do you treat the process of naming so casually that you don't even think about yours, and how it came about? More significantly, how do you process and decide on a name for your child, as a parent? To be fair to people, in general, expectedly, we don't have a choice in our names and naming. We have seen cases where people change their names when and where they have the rights to do so. Invariably, such actions also cause significant pains for other parties involved, like the parent/s that gave such names to their children, as they may have had great intentions, best wishes, and prayers tied to such names.

As the author of this book, I took the advantage of the opportunity to really find and document precious information of the meaning, reasons, and contexts associated with my name, Ephraim. Who else is best to provide me with answers than the authors of the name, my parents Jacob and Grace? Why was I named Ephraim? It is not a common name globally. It is not common in my entire family tree across generations. Finally, and most significantly, it has its origin in the Bible in Genesis 41:52 AMP: "He named the second (son) *Ephraim* (fruitfulness), for God has caused me to be fruitful and very successful in the land of my suffering." Why? Jacob and Grace gave me the best explanation and history as much as they could, and I believe they gave it their best shot considering the prevailing circumstances, including the length of time since the naming (and the challenge on their memories), the lack of logic, and their perception of the importance of the information... 'why bother?' Jacob recalled that he was given the name in a dream before I was born. He proceeded accordingly to confirm my name as Ephraim. Grace, understandably, was as perplexed with the process at the time of this narration as she was when the naming was done then.

The fact that I am also a person of the Christian faith, I do believe that the accounts of the Bible are true, and they are of eternal relevance, including our present time. Indeed, I have had a fair bit of "suffering" in my lifetime. However, I must reaffirm my fruitfulness even amid sufferings. Just like her own birth, Grace suffered numerous and unexplained miscarriages prior to giving birth to me. I have also suffered episodes of serious illness over the years. Grace recounted an episode when I was very sick with serious diarrhea almost to the point of death and she took me to various hospitals and yet, there was no improvement. She had literally given up hope and resorted to praying for a

Know your roots and members of your family tree. And as much as reasonably practicable, keep connected.

miracle. She recounted that it was only when I vomited a large worm that I started to mend and recovered fully. Much recently, I had a major bone fracture at 48 years of age. There have been family challenges at "break-point" levels, loss of jobs, etc. Indeed, challenges abound in life. In all these, however, I have turned out to be wiser and more fruitful. I believe in the significance of names.

It is a universally accepted fact: families do not live together forever. Indeed, Jacob's family tree has now spread across the globe including homeland Nigeria, USA, Canada, Switzerland, and Australia.

2.5 Diasporic Connections - Australia

Jacob and Grace have first-generation migrant children in Australia – Ephraim and Joy. Ephraim is married to Esosa, and together, they are blessed with three children – sixteen, thirteen, and eleven years at the time of the publication of this book. Ephraim's sister, Joy, is married to Frederick, and they have two children – eleven and eight years.

Jacob and Grace have visited and had long stays with their children and grandchildren in Australia on two occasions – 2011 and 2019. The voice and wisdom in the content of this book are largely driven by their live experiences during their stay in Australia. They lived with the individual family units of Ephraim and Joy. They interacted with their grandchildren, network of friends, and community members of their children. They visited various shopping centres, places of worships, recreational centres, clinics, and holiday spots. They experienced the weather, the media, infrastructure, financial system (especially insurance), etc. They have been able to draw on their lived experiences, observations, and comparisons, on which they have based their narratives for this book.

The lessons from their narratives being shared in the next couple of sessions is premised on the fact that they are not meant for the author and immediate families alone. The voices and wisdom and the principles therein, are applicable and useful for many others who are interested in the ongoing conversations on better narratives for people in diaspora, sustainable migration and multiculturalism, and the perspectives and voices from home (especially those of parents of first-generation migrants).

Figure 7: Jacob and Grace's Visit to Australia

Reflection 2.0:

- How much do you know about members of your family tree – immediate and extended family members?

____

____

____

- Why do you think it is very important to connect (and keep being connected) to your (family) roots?

____

____

____

If you have not already done so, can you attempt to draw your family tree? You can write your own family story as well.

____

____

____

3.0 Voices from Home: Benefits of Migration

'Skilled migration has clear economic and social benefits for Australia.'

— Amanda Vanstone

'Migration has economic and social benefits for migrants that extend back to their countries of births and heritages.'

— Ephraim Osaghae

Key Words: Economic benefits, social benefits, financial support, family pride, multiculturalism

There have been numerous efforts to challenge the negative stereotypes about people in diaspora which have mostly not been representative, neither have they been progressive. Migrants were always intended to be, and are indeed, part of the solution. They contribute a lot to the countries that have given them the opportunity to resettle and lead successful lives in their new places of residence. They bring significant economic benefits to the nations that have invested in them. Equally important is the fact that they also pass these vast benefits to members of their wider family trees and associated communities across the globe. This chapter re-echoes the voices from home that acknowledge these lasting and deeply appreciated benefits.

3.1 Economic and Social Benefits

Australia is a great example of a country that has managed their migration policies, strategies, and implementation so much better, and it is difficult to overlook the evidence. The growth and wealth of the country have been largely built on the toils and gainful employment of migrants right from the 18th Century, when the first European migrants arrived in the country. Australia has since depended on migrants to work and help develop its vast resources, as well as pay taxes that have ensured the continuous growth of the economy.

Australia has done relatively well in her immigration policies and implementation.

Over the last couple of decades, Australian migration policy has increasingly focused on attracting migrants to fill skill shortages in the country. Indeed, they have excelled in numerous disciplines that enhance the wealth, wellbeing, and growth of nations – medicine, engineering, education, banking and finance, nursing, aged care, the military, IT and technology, aviation, childcare, etc.

Absolutely! Migrants add economic value to nations that provide them with the enabling platforms.

The table below presents a summary of income reported by migrants in Australia during the 2013-14 financial year: approximately $84B – eighty-four billion dollars!

Table 1: Migrant Taxpayers, Total Income By Visa Stream 2013-14 (a)

Visa Stream	Persons No.	Total income(a) $b	Median income $	% of Total income %
Skilled	911 500	61.001	52 892	72.9
Family	413 641	19.167	36 618	22.9
Humanitarian	71 627	2.478	30 277	3.0
Other Permanent	1 056	0.055	42 494	0.1
Provisional	37 440	0.999	22 568	1.2
Total (b)	**1435 264**	**83.701**	**45 200**	**100.0**

(a) In real terms, i.e., income amounts adjusted for Consumer Price Index (CPI).
(b) Includes Visa Stream "Unknown"

This positive trend has continued unto this day. Migrant men, women, and young people are contributing to the economic growth of their new countries. They are driven to succeed. After all, that is why a lot of migrants left their homelands and comfort zones in pursuit of survival, success, and meaningful impacts, as applicable. Nations like Australia have done their parts by accepting or inviting these migrants, where applicable, to contribute to the growth of their countries while giving the migrants themselves the opportunity to procure economic benefits for themselves and their dependents as well. Such dependents will usually extend beyond their current residences and even citizenships in diaspora, to their homelands. Migration indeed has become a vehicle for wealth creation for all stakeholders involved – their new countries, their countries of birth, and, maybe most significantly for many migrants, their families – firstly, their immediate family units, and by association and family trees, their dependents back in their homelands. This was evident in the testimony of the narrators and main characters of this book.

> **Many migrants work very hard to care for immediate and extended families.**

Jacob and Grace have observed the difference between the situations in diaspora and back home based on extended visits to Australia on two occasions. They have seen how their first-generation migrant children are driven to work hard and seize all available opportunities to create wealth. They have even expressed concerns that "they work too hard."

Indeed, many migrants lacked the opportunities for work, career, and potential for wealth back in their home countries. This is one of the common reasons for migration in the first place. They take the giant leap of leaving family and the "comfort zone" of their place of upbringing and migrating to a new country in pursuit of 'greener pastures.' Thus, given the opportunities, they really work hard and earn hard. Thankfully, they have ended up being better off economically.

The economic benefits of migration are particularly evident when the status of people in diaspora are compared to equivalent scenario back in their country of birth. The exchange rates for foreign currencies have largely contributed to the advantageous position. In the case of Nigeria, as an example, one Aussie dollar can procure much more equivalent product/service worth between N150 to N250 (Nigerian Naira) for most parts of the last decade (see Figure 8 for some historical data). The implication of this situation is that one dollar earned here in Australia can procure much more back in homeland Nigeria. Indeed, this is a similar situation in other countries in similar contexts. A migrant in diaspora Australia would have more economic and

Foreign exchange rates have largely favoured many migrants in more economically stable countries however unsustainable this may be on the long run.

spending power to provide support to family members back in their country of birth, for example.

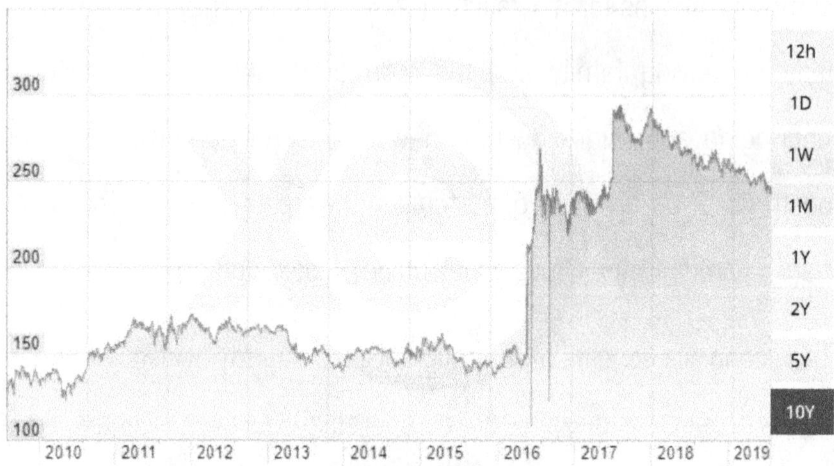

Figure 8: Historical Trend of AUD/NGN Currency Exchange Rates for past 10 years (www.xe.com)

Thus, many established migrants will seek to create wealth in their new countries of residence in the first instance. However, they also seize the opportunities to build investments back in their home countries – real estate, educational facilities, shares, etc. with the hope that such diversity of investments can lead to wealth creation over time. This prospect is largely enhanced by the significant differences in foreign exchange rates as shown in Figure 8 above. The author, as well as Jacob and Grace, are not financial advisers or even close to being experts in that regard. Indeed, readers should seek the right advice on such financial matters, including investments. However, they have seen enough cases and trends to suggest the economic benefits of migration in this regard.

There is another indirect benefit for parents and family members of first-generation migrants back home. They have developed positive feelings of their children in diaspora when they see and participate in these investments. Moreover, there are real and perceived expectations that with such assets in their homelands, their children will regularly come back home to check out their investments. Whether those outcomes remain perceived or real depends on individual groups of parents (and extended families) and their first-generation migrant children in diaspora. Nevertheless, the benefits of migration for members of the family tree are real. There is also little or no doubt that the impacts are felt back home, sometimes where it matters most. This is particularly true regarding support for family, pride in the community, and multiculturalism.

3.2 Support for Family

First-generation migrants provide significant support for their parents and family members back in their countries of birth. This includes direct provision of cash for everyday care and living expenses, support with business set-up and entrepreneurship, and pursuit of high-quality education, including the option of overseas studies (again, joining the diaspora). Prospects for overseas trips are another set of economic benefits of migration. These are just like the types that Jacob and Grace enjoyed. Thankfully, in their case, it also triggered the idea and implementation of the project that has resulted in this book and great resource material.

Such trips overseas, many times, with all expenses paid from origin to destination, return. There are also opportunities for shopping, medical care, tourism, and even paid work, where applicable. This is a breakthrough for family members in developing nations, including those still dealing with significant levels of poverty. Oversea trips are luxurious adventures. Thus, they were previously reserved for the wealthy, diplomats, government officials, politicians, and national contingents for international sporting events (commonwealth games, Olympics, etc.). Parents of first-generation migrants can now enjoy the benefits of such trips and associated feelings of well-being and pride.

> **First-generation migrants provide significant support for their parents and family members back in their countries of birth.**

However, such supports for family members have triggered conflicts and tensions between first-generation migrants and family members back in their home country and, sometimes, even in the current country of residence.

In most situations, the first-generation migrants work very hard to raise funds for developing and establishing such investments. Of course, this is in addition to the priority of raising and caring for their immediate family unit in their current places of residence in diaspora. Firstly, and unfortunately, there are numerous cases where the investments are not well managed and many occasions, they become failed investments with outstanding debts to be paid. More disturbingly, there are cases where such mismanagement and/or failures are predictable; family members have the beliefs and expectations that first-generation migrants in diaspora (owner-relatives of such investments) are already "made," they are better-off, and do not need the anticipated benefits from the investments. Thus, they care very little about the investments/assets in their care and hardly assume the level of responsibilities required to ensure success. There have been reports where such situations proceed to worse scenarios like verbal and physical abuse, unlawful dispossession, and threats of harm if the asset owners (first-generation migrants in diaspora) come physically to try and re-possess their assets. Indeed, there are situations where these have resulted in long-term injury and deaths, unfortunately. Moreover, the asset owners will hardly be able to take trips to their home countries to "pick up a fight" and attempt to defend and/or repossess their rightful assets. This is coupled with the reality that, more often, there are no established legal and record-keeping institutional frameworks to support such a fight for justice. Many migrants are now increasingly exploring alternative locations and more fluid assets for investments while they keep exploring other means of retaining connections with their home countries and family members.

Migrants and family members can keep working together to ensure continuation of support for dependents despite associated challenges. After all, conflicts are inevitable even in family contexts.

One key root cause of such issues is set expectations, which are also tied to cultural norms associated with the upbringing and heritages of many migrants in diaspora. It is generally believed in the African context, for example, that a man (or woman) does not just care for their immediate family alone but rather he or she belongs to a family tree that extends beyond his or her "small" family unit. There is also another norm closely tied to this: once you proceed and live "abroad," i.e., in diaspora, you are well off and should be able to respond to every financial challenge back home. There are situations where first-generation migrants have sponsored members of their extended families in setting up businesses or further education, including cases where they join them in the current country of residence. Unfortunately, these have not gone very well for many cases. Still tied to that root of expectation is that the "big brother or sister" should be responsible for their ongoing financial well-being. Thus, rather than build on the advantages of the initial financial support and consolidate and build on from that platform provided, they keep depending on ongoing support and rescue. Unfortunately, many times, the "big brother or sister" is also struggling to survive, get established, and keep the balance in an already tough situation of the *struggle in the middle* of people in diaspora. There is a need to state that this is not the case for every first-generation migrant in diaspora. Neither is this generalizable for every family. But the point needed to be made and, hopefully, this will be wisdom for a few.

Thankfully, the case of Jacob and Grace and their first-generation migrant children in Australia has been mostly positive, including acknowledgment of the benefits of financial support, pride in the community, and they have embodied the additional benefits of multiculturalism that result from having members of the family in diaspora.

3.3 Pride in the Community

Jacob and Grace clearly articulated the pride they enjoy in the community as a result of having children in diaspora, firstly, the feeling of satisfaction that their first-generation migrant children are settled very well in their new countries of residence. They have visited and stayed with family members in the USA and Australia, and they feel blessed to be part of the diasporic journey and narrative. They have enjoyed the beauties of both worlds, as well as the capacity to fly over continents, visit places of interest, and interact with their children, grandchildren, as well as many friends and neighbours from various cultures.

During their last trip to Perth, Australia, Jacob and Grace went to many places of interest, including popular holiday spots like Busselton and Margaret River. There were many family catch-up times, as well as the pride of spending quality moments and memories to keep for life.

Back home, Jacob and Grace have also enjoyed the acknowledgement and admiration from friends, neighbours, and the wider community, which has further added to the feeling of pride and fulfilment for them. Yes, they will still have to readjust to life over there, and they have. However, the memories have remained with them. Other family members of the first-generation migrants, especially their siblings, have also expressed appreciation for the care and experience given to their parents, Jacob and Grace.

This positive feeling is even more significant for aging parents and family members, where applicable. This was the case with Jacob and Grace, as they were in their 70s and 80s, respectively, during their last visit to Australia. Indeed, they were becoming quite frail with age, along with some age-related sicknesses, to the extent that there was some initial doubt that they would be able to fly. It is wise to *hit the iron while it is still hot*. This is one area of our lives that should suffer the negative impact of procrastination.

First-generation migrants should give their parents and other significant family members the experience that would afford them such sense of pride and well-being. There are expenses involved, and there may be a valid argument that this may be unaffordable in some cases. They include cost of visa applications and preparations, medical examinations, road and air flights (back in the home country and overseas), and hotel accommodations, especially during transit, where applicable. The other significant costs, sometimes overlooked, are associated with all the required adjustments of their first-generation migrant children and their families, including the need to take time off work, extra expenses, cost of entertainment, and creating memories.

Migrants can continue to give their parents and other family members the experience that would afford them some sense of pride and well-being.

The case of Jacob and Grace is in direct perspective for this book. The benefits far outweigh the costs. The pride and fulfilment from the experience remain with Jacob and Grace, their first-generation migrant children, other siblings in the family, and the immediate community of friends back home and here in Australia. For the author: "I will do this all over again, though there are lessons learned that will be implemented in order to make it even more enjoyable for my parents, myself and immediate family, and my sister and her immediate family as well. I will write more stories, bigger stories, with wider and deeper impacts."

Reflection 3.0:

- How has migration been of benefits to you? This may be from any view point applicable to you – a migrant or someone of migrant background, a non-migrant, a service provider, a policy maker, etc.

  ____

  ____

  ____

- How do you support your family (immediate and extended)? It may not be financial support sometimes.

  ____

  ____

  ____

4.0 Challenges of Migration and Wisdom from Our Roots

'A broken immigration system means broken families and broken lives.'

— Jose Antonio Vargas

'Choices are the hinges of destiny'

— Edwin Markham

Key Words: Cost of migration, children and grandchildren, cultural norms, cultural conflicts, family roots

Migration has massive benefits for countries like Australia that have embraced people from all over the globe. As presented in the previous chapter, the economic and social benefits to the countries, the migrants themselves, their immediate and extended families in their country of residence, as well as those back home. However, it is becoming increasingly acknowledged that migration also comes with its costs. The costs are more than financial – including cost of migration visa applications and preparations, medical examinations, road and air flights (back in the home country and overseas), and hotel accommodations, especially during transit, where applicable. More often, these costs are further multiplied depending on the number of people in the migrating family. The entire subject of cost of migration cannot be completely discussed in one book. A few of them will be highlighted in this chapter. These are mostly the softer and social aspects of the cost of migration. They are presented from the viewpoints of parents of first-generation migrants – based on their experiences during extended visits on two occasions as well as ongoing engagement over the years with their families in diaspora.

4.1 The Issue of Distance and Time: "Out of Sight is Out of Mind"

Many migrants treasure memories of their upbringing back in their countries of birth. They regularly recollect episodes, periods, and events with people that were associated with these histories of their journeys in life, including immediate and extended family members. They fondly reflect on how they have shared life and social interactions with loved ones in the earlier part of their lives. They shared family celebrations, cultural norms, and strong friendships.

Over time and distance, these bonds and relationships become very weak and they snap. More often, the severances are not due to lack of efforts on both sides. Rather, migrants incur significant expenses to maintain connections and keep in touch with families and friends back in their countries of birth. Where they can afford it, and depending on their visa conditions, some have embarked on regular trips back to their homelands which include airfares, accommodations, etc. Others use technologies like Skype, Zoom, FaceTime, or traditional telephone calls. A few are privileged to have many extended family members in the new country; they organise regular get-togethers, especially around festive periods, special celebrations (birthdays, anniversaries, etc.), and public holidays. Indeed, such investments do yield good and lasting dividends. But too soon, the reality sets in despite the efforts: *out of sight is out of mind.*

> **This is the reality of life in diaspora with regards to connections to our roots: "out of sight is out of mind"**
>
> **Migrants can keep bridging the gap as much as reasonably**

People in diaspora usually experience mixed feelings in response to the reality of losing connections and networks back in their countries of birth and upbringing. Sometimes, there is a sense of loss. Other instances, people approach the issue as something that was meant to happen. After all, there is an African proverb that states: *families do not live together, forever.* On most occasions, migrants pull themselves together, reassure themselves of the *whys* associated with their migration in the first instance, and push on.

Migration has significantly changed the dynamics of family and connectedness to their roots, many times, forever. People in diaspora go through life reinvention several times depending on individual experiences, good or bad; hopefully, more of the former. One can almost draw an analogy of this situation to the claim that a cat has nine lives. It is further explained in the ancient proverb that for three of those years, the cat plays, for another three he strays, and for the last three he stays. This portrays some level of dexterity and agility that people in diaspora have typically become known to display in their journeys of life.

Parents of first-generation migrants feel the impact of gaps in distance and relationship with their children and grandchildren over time. This is particularly challenging in the growing and very serious issue of loneliness in the whole world. These parents want to be able to relate more with their children as they grow older. The situation is not as easy for migrants in diaspora themselves. One painful experience that has been known within the circles of people in this context is not to be able to be by the bedside of dying parents or loved ones back in their country of birth. Some are not able to attend funeral ceremonies of such loved ones to pay their last respects. This situation is further challenging for cultures where these rites are significant, and many migrants bear the burden of such loss of precious moments in their hearts over a long period of time and may not have received closure to such pains with loved ones. We should not add to the negative statistics. Let's challenge the negativity associated with the construct around otherness in this context. Yes, this is not to promote dropping all our guards as custodians of our own family values and way of life. But rather, this is promoting the benefits of sharing lives, community, and an extended family system. Various community groups have the potential to fill this gap for their members, as much as reasonably possible.

The main message of this section is not to devalue to benefits of migration and the better life that most people in diaspora enjoy in their new places of residence. Indeed, host countries have been open-minded and gracious to embrace people into their living space and domain. This, indeed, should not be taken for granted. Rather, the issue must be acknowledged, discussed, and validated. Hopefully, the main characters in the setting – parents of first-generation migrants and migrants themselves – should undertake measures to make it easier for themselves. Indeed, life must be lived. We must embrace the spaces and times that we occupy at different stages in our lives. Maybe it is okay to be like the cat – we can play a bit, stray a bit, and stay in the moments. This does not take away the responsibilities to relationships, especially those related to families and our roots. Our stability comes from the roots, and we must care for them. We must nurture our roots. Many times, it costs money and time. But a strong root system is worth every investment!

4.2 Weakening Connections with Children and Grandchildren

The challenge of weakening connections with children and grandchildren is partly connected to the issue of distance and time discussed in the previous section. Parents of first-generation migrants increasingly experience loss of relationship with their migrant children. This gets worse with grandchildren and further generations in their lineage, and this can hardly be linked to a fault on the part of any one party involved. As already mentioned, it is largely attributed to distance and time and the fact that people lead different lives in countries and cultures that are thousands of miles apart.

It seems to be getting worse with the already prevalent loss of family connections even among migrant families themselves as they settle into their new countries. The challenges of trying to retain relationships and connections within immediate families in the new countries are widely acknowledged. Incidences of domestic violence (DV) in migrant families are a growing concern for governments and community leaders. The causes of this negative trend are varied and challenging enough in themselves to deserve a separate focus. Understandably, people in diaspora may have become less concerned about the growing gaps in connections with more distant family members, including parents and other family members. But avoidance does not take away the associated pains and strategic impacts of weakening connectedness to our roots. This situation affects both sides.

> **Weak connections between parents back home and children/ grandchildren in diaspora:**
> **it is primarily no one's fault but part of the cost of migration; all parties can keep working together to bridge the gap.**

Parents of first-generation migrants who would have loved to have been very connected to their children and grandchildren experience the loss of care and joy of the relationships. Usually, it is the joy of every grandparent to receive a call from his or her grandchild to say hello. His or her day would have been so enriched with such event. How about receiving a gift from a grandchild? They might remark with moments like: "You have added more days to my years of living." How wise it will be if first-generation migrant children (and their own children) still pick up the phone to seek counsel from their parents back in their countries of birth. Yes, they may not be able to relate to every context associated with new countries of their migrant children. Indeed, there are some differences in economic, social, and cultural norms between new countries of residences of people in diaspora and those of their births that may further complicate the challenges. But parents back in countries of birth do have the wisdom to share, as well as the good of members of their family trees at heart. They have a stake in the success and progress of their descendants. Could the lack or weakening strength of this connectedness to our roots have contributed to the growing ills in families and society at large? Again, it goes back to the need for stability in individuals, families, and the community. Strong roots will support stability.

It is wise to acknowledge that there are no quick fixes to the challenge of weakening connections to our roots. This is even more challenging. But we can start from little things. Like the popular saying goes: little drops make the ocean. Start by making more of those calls, often.

Grandchildren can, as well. It starts from the awareness that we all need healthy roots for our own overall well-being.

4.3 Cultural Norms

A culture is the set of customs, traditions, and values of a society or community, such as an ethnic group, a soccer club, or a nation (www.wikipedia.org). But culture has become as numerous and varied as human beings. Indeed, there is room for multiculturalism and the value that it brings. For example, Australia is a multicultural country with residents who identify with more than 270 ancestries (www.humanrights.gov.au). Other statistics as shown in Figure 9 include the fact that one in four are born overseas and one in two have at least one parent born overseas. It is obvious that there shall be challenges regarding cultural norms with such multicultural context. The situation is not unique to Australia.

> **"A nation's culture resides in the hearts and in the soul of its people." - Mahatma Gandhi**

We can peacefully coexist with mutual respect between different cultures inhabiting the same communities, nations, and the world at large. Yet we can (and should) be aware of some cultural norms that are associated with different groups which they have known and acquired over time. Yes, these differences have been known to cause divisions and conflicts in families, communities, neighbourhoods, and even nations. But it should not. Rather, an awareness of these cultures within a multicultural context should provide information for all parties to learn and appreciate one another and thus foster the benefits of multiculturalism.

> **"We experience new culture with every journey."**
> **— Lailah Gifty Akita**

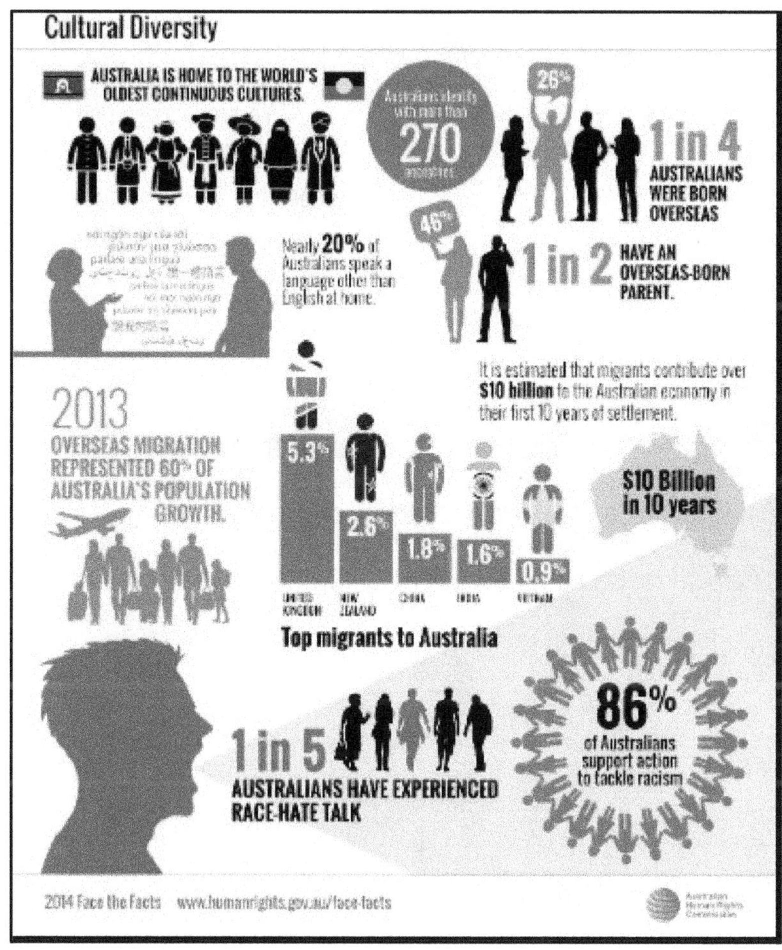

Figure 9: Facts and Figures about Multicultural Australia (www.humanrights.gov.au)

Some of these cultural norms are presented below. Again, they are based on the narrations of Jacob and Grace, especially regarding their own interactions with their children and grandchildren, friends of their children, as well as lessons learned during their extended stays in Australia. The point also needs to be made that their stories are not generalizable to all cultures and people. However, the principles remain the same: the more I am aware of other people's cultures, the more I will appreciate the similarities and differences, the more, hopefully, the knowledge will help us respect the views and backgrounds of others and live well together.

> **"We are increasingly recognising and accepting, respecting and celebrating, our cultural diversity" Julie Bishop**

4.3.1 Food

Food is one classical way of expressing multiculturalism. There are different recipes for food within families, communities, and around the world. In Australia, for example, there are so many varieties of food that reflect the different cultures associated with the over 270 ancestries (refer to Figure 2 above). They will include bush tuckers (which are native to Australian Aboriginal people), Australian hotdogs, American burgers, British pies, Caribbean fish stew, Indian masala chicken, Italian pasta, Japanese sushi, Chinese sea bass, Nigerian moi-moi, French ratatouille, Mexican tacos, Thai curries, etc. These varieties of food will look, feel, smell, and taste different. Yet, they are savouries for people that know and eat them very well. Over time, people have learnt to taste and, sometimes, really enjoy new food. It is one medium for interaction with other cultures.

However, it is a challenge for some people, including parents of first-generation migrants, when they visit with families in diaspora. It is unexpected that people will change the type of food they've lived on over the years. Some adjust and others, not so well. It is particularly difficult for some cases that the situation has become a constraint for the length of their visits or even visiting at all. Thankfully, several cultural groups have started setting up culturally aligned grocery shops where they can buy foods that are common with their cultures. For such communities or nationals with significant population, this type of business has now become a very viable option for employment and entrepreneurship.

The issue of food has not really been a significant challenge for Jacob and Grace. In one regard, they have adjusted to eating a few varieties, including trying new options. Where it went down well, they tried a bit more and got to like such options. They never got around hotdogs though.

Just like many other aspects of multiculturalism, diversity in food should not cause conflicts. We can appreciate difference in a positive way. Yes, we may not like the look, smell, or taste of some food types, but we must learn to appreciate the difference and decline respectfully where applicable.

4.3.2 Fashion

Fashion, just like food, is very diverse, even in the family context. It becomes even more varied at the community and national levels. Again, this can become a source of conflict for people in diaspora, especially for migrants with upbringing in a collectivist culture coming into an egalitarian country like Australia. For the latter, many aspects of life, including what you choose to wear (or not wear), is so much unrestricted and left to you to choose.

The challenge can be further compounded when some additional cultural and religious beliefs prescribe what is acceptable to wear within the family and in the community. This situation has been a common trigger for conflicts and, unfortunately, could lead to domestic violence. Consider an example of a first-generation migrant couple of North African and very religious backgrounds with two teenage children – a boy and a girl who were born and have so far been raised in Australia. The girl decides at some point that she would like to wear mini-skirts in public like her other friends in school. Another scenario is a situation where the boy tells the parents that he wants to pierce his ear (maybe even both) and start wearing earrings just like some of his friends.

These two scenarios that portray clash of cultures are very common causes of conflicts, especially within migrant family units. It even becomes more complicated when parents of such first-generation migrants are visiting with them and get involved in such scenarios. Coming from a collectivist culture and possibly a patriarchal system, they would feel it is their right to get into it and *put their grandchildren in their rightful places*. Unfortunately, it does not work that way, most often. How can such situations be handled in such a way that there is no violence, and no one ends up in jail? Who is responsible for the cause of these growing differences in the first instance? Could it be that the culture of the first-generation migrant parents has become too archaic and needs to be over-written with a more "modern culture" – like an egalitarian culture?

More often, no one is to be blamed for such conflicts. Not the children who are born into one era and prevailing culture, have parents who have grown up in another, and who have peers who have so much influence on their actions. After all, who does not want to belong to a group? Patience is very necessary. Unfortunately, many migrants in diaspora have learnt the hard way. They have taken actions before thinking about the law and impacts of their actions.

Such situations demand wisdom – doing the right things, rightly. The two must go together as much as possible. A parent can be firm (parenting) without violence (lawfully), as hard as it is, sometimes. It increasingly comes down to negotiation. Grandparents will also require some advance induction as well. Again, this would have to be done rightly – respectfully – otherwise, first-generation migrants may also be in trouble with the extended family. It is difficult to maintain the balance sometimes. But it is something that must be done and done rightly. So much is at stake, most of the time.

4.3.3 Raising Children and Discipline in Homes

Raising children and discipline in homes are another set of cultural norms that are known to challenge migrant families in diaspora. Who is responsible for raising children and for enforcing discipline in the home? It is implied that parents are responsible. However, discipline must be done within the boundaries of the law. This is where it has become very tricky for first-generation migrants. For example, it is still difficult adjusting to the attitude of younger people regarding manner of greetings and respect for elders. Style of discipline is another challenge. Many have grown up in cultures that promote some form of physical "punishments" as disciplinary measures. Examples include commanding offending children to kneel for a certain period. The principle with this method is that the pain and humiliation will serve as a deterrent from offending in the future. It was also a regular disciplinary practice to be beaten with sticks on the hand several times to ensure that the pain gets to the offender. Arguably, it worked in that culture. There could also a further argument that such disciplinary styles should work even in an egalitarian society like Australia. Indeed, some will even claim that the absence of such punitive measures could be the reason for the breakdown of orderliness within families and homes.

Indeed, one will almost certainly go to jail for abuse of one's own child if any of the disciplinary measures described above are implemented in a place like Australia. It is almost certain that any of such actions that result in injury to a child (visible or emotional) will be taken up by the right authorities. Usually, the 'intelligence network' of neighbours, peers, school teachers, child support workers, doctors, and anyone within reach of the child in this situation will pick it up and escalate the situation to the relevant authorities for swift actions. Many times, it does not go well for the parent in the situation. This is where many first-generation migrants get into trouble with the law. Unfortunately, many are taken on a pathway they never envisaged for themselves or any member of their families. There have been such cases where what a parent may have considered 'my responsibility to put my house in order' ended in a jail term and criminal record due to clash of cultural norms and the law. Is it worth it? Meanwhile, the family that was supposedly being 'protected' would end up being exposed to greater dangers with the absence of the parent. Again, wisdom is required – doing the right things, rightly. First-generation migrants will require patience, negotiation, and emotional intelligence to navigate this path for some hope of coming out on the other side as one happy family unit.

Parents of first-generation migrants would most likely have sanctioned the disciplinary actions described earlier on. There could be cases where they would undertake the actions themselves, if not restrained. Hopefully, they would not like to go to jail, neither would they like their children to be incarcerated. Jacob and Grace get this point. They have heeded their children's counsel over time, particularly regarding the law and cultural norms that may have been okay back at home and did work for them (the first-generation migrants), but they may not be applicable to their grandchildren. They respected the boundaries even though they did not agree with some of the laws.

There are numerous researches and publications on the best discipline for children, and some of them are specific to various cultures. What really works? What is best for the children, their families, and the wider community?

4.3.4 Marriages and Marital Norms

Marriage and marital norms are another set of challenges for first-generation migrants in diaspora. The impact of this one flows on to generations down the track. This is one that may be difficult to discuss without triggering the suspicion of bias, considering the author's male gender. However, opening value-adding conversations around the issues associated with this aspect of a migrant's journey is worth the risk. Sub-topics of interest and relevance are numerous. However, three of them are discussed further below. The aim is not to prescribe or take sides; there are qualified counsellors for that purpose. Rather, some key points will be presented from the lenses of Jacob and Grace, who are of African backgrounds. Hopefully, some wisdom will be available for readers, where applicable.

"Democracy" in Homes

Hopefully, it has become clear to most first-generation migrants that we cannot continue or do marriage and family like we did back in our countries of birth. For example, most parts of Africa practice the paratracheal marriage system. The man is the first and final authority. It is not a democracy. Then we come into an egalitarian society like Australia, where it is more of the latter. Unfortunately, many first-generation migrant men are only adjusting after much suffering of the impacts of holding on to the cultural norms that they have grown up with and that some married into (psychological contract) before migration. The real question has mostly come down to this: do you want a marriage/family or not? If yes, adjust... and suffer the consequences of swallowing your pride. If no, then be ready to move on alone… and suffer the consequences of unplanned singleness. The other alternative which is least chosen: go back to your country of birth where the type of marriage you want really works. Even with that, be ready to go back alone. This may sound blunt. But this is the type of approach that this situation demands. Moreover, people coming behind on the same pathway need to know the facts, learn fast, and be wiser. Again, the wisdom that would most likely work for first-generation migrants is like most of the aspects already discussed: patience, negotiation, emotional intelligence.

Extended Families

Different cultures treat extended family systems differently and this can be another challenging aspect for first-generation migrants in diaspora. For example, it is a strongly held view in many parts of Africa that when you marry a person, you are not only "married" or committed to that person only but, rather, to all the members of the person's family tree – extended family. This is typical of a collectivist society. Not so with an egalitarian one. Thus, this situation becomes a challenge for the migrant who is not able to adjust to the reality. Solution? Appreciation of the difference, negotiation, and adjustments.

Conflict Resolution

Collectivist culture: If we have a challenge in our marriage, we need to consult with "elders" in our extended family so they can provide us with some guidance to help us get back unto the 'right' pathway. Everyone in the family has a stake in ensuring the continuation of that marriage. This is even more important in a culture where separation and divorce are a thing of 'shame' to the family. Thus, there is a collective interest in resolving the conflict and ensuring that the couple stay together, however together they really are.

Individualistic culture: If the marriage is not working, move on. It is not the business of any third party. Extended family members may only be aware of the separation or divorce after the paperwork is done.

Objectively, which is better? What are the dynamics for first-generation migrants? Which is better if children are involved? How far should we go to resolve marital conflicts?

Different Marital Systems (Same-Sex Marriage, De Facto, etc.)

First-generation migrants in diaspora are exposed to and do have to deal with the fast-paced changing landscape of marriage when they leave the world they have traditionally known from childbirth. In Australia, as an example, a de facto relationship is one in which a couple lives together on a legally recognized basis and they enjoy rights regarding child benefits, separation, property settlement, and child maintenance as typically dealt with under the Family Law. Many migrants get confused about such situations and do have to undertake fast-track self-education to understand such difference in what they have always known marriage to mean. At least, this will help them avoid being on the wrong side of the law of the land.

Unfortunately, many parents of first-generation migrants may never be able to wrap their heads and minds around such differences. Their children will have to take on the role of shielding them for possible exposure to conflicts and litigation that may arise out of ignorance in dealing with couples in such relationships.

Same-sex marriage is more recent and tensely debated in most countries. It has become legally recognized in some countries. The case of Australia is still quite fresh as at the time of writing this book. The country had a plebiscite (12 Sep to 7 Nov 2017) – a nationwide vote to gauge public feedback on marriage equality, i.e., gay marriage will be equally recognized by the law just like traditional marriage between a man and a woman. The yes vote was more than the no and Australia has since signed it into law. For many first-generation migrants, this is another aspect of their new countries, where applicable, that they must seek to understand the ramifications fast. Otherwise, they can commit a criminal offence without knowing it. It could just be an allegation of discrimination when they are just sticking to the only construct of marriage that they have always known. There is need for education and awareness, especially for new and emerging members of various migrant communities.

For first-generation migrants that are not yet married: hopefully, the above situation does not paint a gloomy picture for marriage in diaspora. Rather, consider the points above as more information to help you decide wisely. Good luck!

4.3.5 Aging and Death

The need for children to care for their aging parents is an important cultural norm in many migrant communities. It is appreciated that many first-generation migrants make adequate financial provisions for their care, especially considering the advantages of favourable foreign exchange, as highlighted in chapter three. There are also efforts to keep in touch via telephone and, in some rare situations, they make additional investments in regular visits, etc. However, the aging parents need their physical presence, touch, and companionship in most of the cases during this phase of their lives.

The phase of dying is even more traumatic for both sides, most of the time. This is especially relevant when dying parents of migrants are given the opportunity of predictable dying experience. Examples of these include being in hospital or at home while going through the final phase of death. They would prefer not to miss out on the significance of having their children by their bedside during the final period. Their children, on the other hand, would always feel this sense of indebtedness to themselves and to their parents to be at their bedside during such periods. They would like to provide comfort and some assurances, where possible and applicable, respectively. They would like to have a chat with them. Many times, such conversations are cherished, as they would have carried much significance for them and their children, etc. They would have loved to be just there and be part of the solemn moments with their parents. These are priceless and will always be

> **Differences in family roots, heritages and cultural norms can be positively appreciated and respected in the spirit of sustainable multiculturalism.**
>
> **— Lailah Gifty Akita**

part of the conversations around what is being missed as a result of migration.

Many first-generation migrants also miss out in participating in funeral ceremonies and other traditional norms in honour of their departed parents back in their country of birth. Several factors are usually associated with this situation. Firstly, the migrants are still trying to settle into the new country and may not have the necessary visa that will give him or her (or their families) the right to travel to their countries of birth for the funeral, and still be able to come back into the new country of residence. Secondly, they may not be able to afford the trip and all that is required of them, financially.

Death and funeral rites may mean much more in some cultures than others. Again, the differences can be positively appreciated and respected in the spirit of sustainable multiculturalism.

Reflection 4.0:

- How are you dealing with the situation of "out of sight is out of mind" regarding close friends and family members that are far away?

  ____

  ____

  ____

- How do we foster connections between second-generation migrants and their extended family members especially those back in their parents' country of birth (their roots)?

  ____

  ____

  ____

- Which of the cultural norms of our forefathers should we retain now that we reside in a new country? How do we foster more appreciation and respect for other cultures in a multicultural country like Australia?

  ____

  ____

  ____

5.0 Implications for Stakeholders

"A nation's culture resides in the hearts and in the soul of its people."

- Mahatma Gandhi

'I may not have gone where I intended to go, but I think I have ended up where I intended to be.'

- Douglas Adams

Key Words: Government, Policies, First-Generation Migrants, Parents of First-Generation Migrants

The conversation about migration and people in diaspora should be of interest to all key stakeholders in this context – the migrants in diaspora themselves, government and policy makers in the new country of residence, their counterparts in the country of birth or origin, parents and family members of the migrants, and members of the communities, especially in the new country of residence.

The significance of the family tree and its roots to the well-being of first-generation migrants is hopefully no longer up for debate. There are incentives for all stakeholders to acknowledge the tension of the middle and make it easier for migrants to settle well into their new country of residence. It is also helpful to foster measures that will directly or indirectly ameliorate the challenges associated with migration, including enabling connections of people of migrant backgrounds to their roots. Their economic, social, and mental well-being result in ripple benefits for them, their families (immediate and extended), their host nation, and their communities. Government and policy makers, neighbours and communities, and first-generation migrants themselves all have roles to play in this win-win-win campaign.

5.1 Government and Policy Implications

The Australian government seems to be heeding to the urgency for policies and actions for fostering the connections to the roots as discussed in Chapter 4. Since 2017, the government has announced the introduction of temporary and permanent parent visas for parents of Australians. They will allow Australians to sponsor their parents to stay in Australia for up to five years at a time (temporary option) or permanently join family in Australia.

https://immi.homeaffairs.gov.au/visas/getting-a-visa/visa-finder/join-family – accessed 30 June 2019

This means applying for parents of first-generation migrants must be outside Australia when they apply, they must have an eligible child who is a settled Australian citizen or permanent resident, must meet the balance-of-family test, and must have an Assurance of Financial Support (some of the options require relatively high visa fees).

It is heartwarming that relevant governments are recognising the importance of the connectedness between migrants and their family trees and roots.

With some of the visas, the parent of the first-generation migrant can work and study in Australia, and maybe, more significantly, he or she can enroll in Australia's public health care scheme, Medicare.

Visiting visas – Tourist or sponsored family streams are the most popular types of temporary visas in Australia. The tourist visa lets the holder visit Australia as a tourist, to go on a cruise, or to see family and friends. The sponsored family visa stream, on the other hand, lets people who are sponsored, usually by a family member, come to Australia to visit their family members. Visiting parents can stay up to

12 months with any of these visas. They cost much less and there is less processing time as well.

The visa is designed to allow the parents of Australians to spend longer periods of time with their children in Australia *without placing additional burden on Australia's health care system*. Many migrants would have been waiting for such opportunity to reconnect with parents and enjoy the benefits of having them live with them and be very close to the family, including grandchildren.

However, many will still miss out due to the high visa application fee, as well as possible challenge in passing the medical test. After all, these parents require your care when they face health challenges. There is also some sense in ensuring that such gesture by the government does not result in *too much* burden on Australia's health care system.

This change in policy will be welcomed by many migrants as a right step in the right direction. The cost of inaction is more expensive than the associated costs with this latest policy change by the government. Nevertheless, the burden should not be left to government alone.

5.2 Multicultural Communities and Migrants in Diaspora

Multiculturalism is no longer a concept to be debated. It is now part of us, globally and nationally. Even most neighbourhoods are increasingly multicultural. Let us acknowledge and celebrate our differences which have been established as having competitive advantages as per a series of practical studies. Indeed, "the uniqueness of individuals is the diversity of life." — Lailah Gifty Akita.

For migrants in diaspora: take advantage of the opportunities being presented by the countries and communities that have embraced you. Stay connected to your roots. Therein lies your stability and long-term productivity. There are four recurring key themes in the previous chapter and virtually the whole of this book: succeeding in diaspora, wisdom, patience, negotiation, sustainable multiculturalism, intergenerational benefits, and forward-focused changes.

Reflection 5.0:

- What more could first-generation migrants do to ensure smoother and sustainable settlement for themselves and their immediate families while maintaining connections with their roots?

- What more could governments do with regards to migration policies and implementation in order to foster sustainable integration of migrants and people of migrant backgrounds?

- What more could other stakeholders do in the context of migrant settlement in order to support sustainable multicultural communities?

6.0 Concluding Remarks

There is a saying: *no man is an island*. Man, in this context could mean man, woman, youth or even a child. The point being made with this proverb is this context is the reality that people generally do not do so well alone. We do relatively better in connectedness, in families, and in communities. This book has highlighted the importance and urgency for people, especially migrants in diaspora and people of migrant backgrounds, to make efforts to maintain connection with their roots including members of their families – near and far.

Voices from home is not necessarily about Jacob and Grace. Yes, they have contributed their voice to this timely subject on challenges of people in diaspora and particularly first-generation migrants. Rather, this book will hopefully trigger further attention on the importance of including the extended family structure and roots in the conversations around sustainable settlement of migrants and people of migrant backgrounds. It is no longer enough just to throw funds at issues of integration of migrants into the mainstream of the communities and nations of their new countries.

Key stakeholders including migrants and people of migrant backgrounds themselves, government and policy makers, service providers, and relevant members of the community, need to look beyond just the immediate if we must ensure sustainable solutions for value-adding settlement. It is imperative to also consider migrant roots and voices from home. This strategy is even more relevant when developing solutions for engaging youth of migrant backgrounds in helping them to chart courses for meaningful whole-life experience in their new countries of residence.

Parents of first-generation migrants have a significant role to play as well and there is an urgent need to foster the mechanism for establishing significant and life-long connection with their children and descendants in diaspora. Thankfully, some forward-thinking governments like Australia have started taking some responsibilities and leadership in this regard with favourable migration laws that will support the capacity for parents to join their children in diaspora on a long-term and even permanent basis depending on the visa requirements. This is great help! Hopefully, migrants themselves and their applicable family members can see the value and take full advantage of the opportunity.

The voices from the roots and heritages of migrants in diaspora are so important for multicultural countries like Australia. They will add to the solutions of the challenges associated with multiculturalism. In reality, they may be the only solutions in some instances. With this book, these voices have primarily come through the narration of Jacob and Grace. The details may not be applicable for all situations. However, the principles and wisdom are relevant for most contexts.

You may also be interested in the following books by

Ephraim Osaghae

A HANDBOOK FOR MIGRANTS

The Good, The Challenges, and The Lessons

A Reflective Guide for Meaningful and Whole-Life Experience

A Handbook for Migrants: The Good, The Challenges and The Lessons A Reflective Guide for Meaningful and Whole-Life Experience

Migrants are important contributors to the success and growth of many countries. But they face series of challenges before they can fully attain whole-life balance while integrating into their new countries. These challenges are real, and to some, they have become sources of worry and despair.

As such, each migrant needs all the help that he or she can get. This book provides that, and much more. It is a reflective guide about the beneficial aspects of migration, the social, economic and cultural challenges, as well as associated solutions. All these are presented from a migrant's point of view, and with anecdotes from someone that has walked the path — someone who is keen to share lessons learned so that it will be more comfortable and more rewarding for others, especially those coming behind.

In this book, you will find the following:

- Who really is a migrant?
- The career and business challenges of a migrant; and proposed solutions.

- The challenges and lessons with regards to family life including raising children and youths.
- The essential aspects and preparation for aging and retirement.
- The importance of communities and leadership.
- The lived experiences of a migrant.

You will find great use for the content of this book if you are:

- Intending migrants looking for pre-migration considerations and tips.
- Migrants looking for guidance in work, families, youths and community engagements.
- Non-migrants, students, policymakers, service providers and community leaders.

This book also allows you to participate in meaningful conversations on migrant experiences.

A HANDBOOK

for

MIGRANT YOUTH

PEER TO PEER WISDOM FROM THOSE WHO'VE BEEN THERE, DONE THAT

LiME Youth

Compiled by Ephraim Osaghae

A glimpse into the world of migrant youth
A vibrant group of multicultural youth in Perth, Australia, want you to know what it will take to make it as a young migrant - to live to the fullest, to achieve your dreams and to enjoy the experience. Prepare yourself for insights, stories and lessons from their lives, and the acumen they've gathered from the LiME Project, a friendly conversation to carry with you on this journey.
LiME
ISBN 978-0-6484799-1-8
90000
9 780648 479918

A Handbook for Migrant Youth

Peer To Peer Wisdom From Those Who've Been There, Done That

Contributing Authors: Maria Shyllon, Niche Deng, Esther Batty, Solotin Santana, Gracia Ngandu, Abraham Oyewopo, Joy Ngandu, Fatiha Enilari, Keyshiaa Menezes, Ify Okiwelu, Joshuaa Menezes, Efe Osaghae, Odaro Osaghae, Victor Komaiya, Marcus Wilson, Osamu Ekhator, Saskia Wilson, and King David Oyewopo.

A Glimpse into the World of Migrant Youth. A vibrant group of multicultural youth group presents what it takes to make it as a young migrant - to live to the fullest, to achieve your dreams and to enjoy the experience. Prepare yourself for insights, stories and lessons from their lives, and the acumen they have gathered from the LiME Project.

New and emerging teenagers of migrant backgrounds will find this book particularly useful. Often, lots of support and guidance is available for parents and adults as they become residents of a new country. However, less attention is given to younger migrants. This gap can create detrimental consequences for the youth including social isolation, loss of direction and focus, feeling unsupported and uprooted, helplessness, frustration and irritation due to changes in circumstances, experiencing identity crises, etc.

All young people, migrants as well as those who are already established in the new country will find information in this book very useful. And they can use it to inspire others as well.

Parents, mentors, teachers and school administrators will find valuable tips and suggestions in this book that will help them in their ongoing efforts to make great leaders of their children, mentees and students.

The content in this book will also provide government office holders, policy makers and service providers with real stories and lived experiences from young people themselves.

Finally, while Australia is the context for this book, the principles and lessons are applicable across the globe.

LiME is an initiative of Migrants Professional Bridge Incorporated (MPB) which is also known as Aus-Professional-Bridge (APB).

MPB advances and supports the empowerment, capacity building, and vocational integration of skilled and semi-skilled people of migrant backgrounds enabling them to sustainably participate in socio-economic wellbeing and growth for themselves, their families and Australia.

Some MPB activities include the following:

- Providing networking opportunities and ongoing employment support services to people of migrant backgrounds enabling them to acquire the required local networks and strategies to secure and hold jobs.
- Providing counselling, coaching and mentoring services and support to bridge the gaps caused by lack of suitable capabilities, culture shocks, displacement from career paths, and other such challenges.
- Providing training for up-skilling and/or right-skilling to ensure suitable competencies and qualifications.
- Providing work experience and employment including volunteering opportunities.

- Providing a vehicle for more experienced professionals, philanthropic individuals, groups and organisations to contribute to the cause.
- Facilitating professional integration including career buddy, where applicable.
- Facilitating professionally-aligned programs to engage and empower youths in these disadvantaged communities - "guide them young." LiME is an example of this passion.
- Providing, education / referral, advisory, advocacy, and representation services to people of migrant backgrounds in their bid for a fair go for opportunities and sustainability for their chosen professions.

MPB's Slogan: Facilitating diversity, inclusion & participation . . . providing opportunities for people, businesses and communities.

About The Author

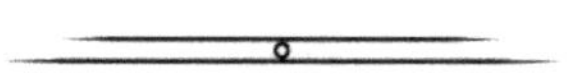

Ephraim Osaghae is the founder and board member of Migrants Professional Bridge Incorporated trading as Aus-Professional-Bridge (APB). He uses his knowledge, skills and passion in leading the team to undertake individual and group engagements including seminars, workshops and programs in educating people and particularly empowering members of migrant communities to lead impactful lives while contributing to national growth. He has led special projects including the 'Adopt / Adapt / Achieve' series, LiME – Leadership in Motion & Experience (for youths 12-17years) and WEWB – Women Empowerment for Work & Business and they have been widely acclaimed as great successes by participants, people in the community, government and private sectors.

Ephraim holds Master's Degrees in Engineering, Business Administration and Business Leadership from renowned universities in Nigeria and Australia. He is also a certified project management professional (PMP®) and Project Business Analysis (PMI-PBA®) from the globally-acclaimed Project Management Institute (PMI). He is director at Tri-W Pty Ltd, a project management and training consulting firm, and teaches project / construction management at Curtin University.

For many years, he has been actively involved in research, education, projects and business management mostly in Africa, Australia and the Middle East. He currently consults, and trains industry groups and students through facilitated learning, professional speaking engagements and conferences across the globe. He is committed to value-adding services, social entrepreneurship and community enrichment.

Ephraim is married to Esosa and they are blessed with three children.

Contact Ephraim:

eosaghae@mpbgroup.org.au

eosaghae@triw.com.au

ephosaghae@gmail.com

www.aus-bridge.org.au

www.triw.com.au

You can also connect via LinkedIn, Twitter, Facebook and Instagram

www.ingramcontent.com/pod-product-compliance
Lightning Source LLC
Chambersburg PA
CBHW062145020426
42334CB00020B/2520

* 9 7 8 0 6 4 8 4 7 9 9 3 2 *